THE DOLLAR BILL
ORIGAMI BOOK

THE DOLLAR BILL
ORIGAMI BOOK

30 Designs That Turn Money into Art

Janessa Munt

Diagrams by Marcio Noguchi

Photographs by Olga Gugnyak and Connor Christensen

Skyhorse Publishing

Skyhorse Publishing books may be purchased in bulk at special discounts for sales promotion, corporate gifts, fund-raising, or educational purposes. Special editions can also be created to specifications. For details, contact the Special Sales Department, Skyhorse Publishing, 307 West 36th Street, 11th Floor, New York, NY 10018 or info@skyhorsepublishing.com.

Skyhorse® and Skyhorse Publishing® are registered trademarks of Skyhorse Publishing, Inc.®, a Delaware corporation.

Visit our website at www.skyhorsepublishing.com.

10 9 8 7 6

Library of Congress Cataloging-in-Publication Data is available on file.

Cover design by Jane Sheppard
Cover photo credit by Olga Gugnyak

Print ISBN: 978-1-5107-0949-2
Ebook ISBN: 978-1-5107-0952-2

Printed in China

Acknowledgments

Steve and Brenda Munt, my parents, who supported and even encouraged my crazy origami habit.

Marcio Noguchi, my wonderful diagrammer, who put in many hours to make this book happen.

Olga Gugnyak, my good friend and photographer for this book.

Table of Contents

$2 Square 9	Airplane 11	Bow 53	Bow Tie 57	Box 1 15	Box 2 17
Bulldog 61	Capricorn 67	Cat Head 19	Crane 73	Norman the Duck 93	Erlenmeyer Flask 23
Fish 27	Goat 77	Heart 31	Lily 33	Manatee 83	Manta Ray 87
Mermaid 129	Pizza Slice 37	Rat 99	Sailboat 41	Seal 105	Shooting Star 133
Simple Bird 45	Snake 111	T. Rex 137	Tulip 49	Turkey 115	Walrus 121

Introduction

After learning how to fold an origami box at the age of seven, I was hooked. I got any and every origami book I could get my hands on. I folded everything—magazines, newspapers, homework, receipts, and, of course, money.

Once I had mastered folding other people's designs, I started noticing there were animals I wanted to fold that I couldn't find instructions for. I gradually started modifying existing designs to create what I wanted and eventually started designing my very own original origami models.

Now, after years of designing, I have catalogued my dollar bill creations in this book to share with you. I hope you enjoy folding the models as much as I enjoyed designing them.

Supplies

Money

When folding dollar bill origami, you should start with the crispest dollar bills you can find. Banks occasionally carry uncirculated bills, more so around Christmas time. When uncirculated bills are unavailable, bank tellers are usually more than happy to find the newest looking bills for you.

Paper

Often, it is useful to first try folding a model with a piece of paper that is cut to the size ratio of a dollar before attempting the model with a real dollar. To do this, you will need a dollar bill, a sheet of paper, a straight edge, a pencil or pen, and a pair of scissors. Directions on how to easily cut a sheet of paper of any size to the correct size ratio can be found on page 5.

Tools

Dollar bills are relatively thick, and because of this it can be hard to crease through all of the layers. A couple of things that can help are a bone folder and vise grips. A bone folder will ensure that every crease is sharp. It can usually be found in the scrapbooking section of craft stores. Vise grips can help to compress models made up of many layers. They can be found in hardware stores.

Legend

————	Edge	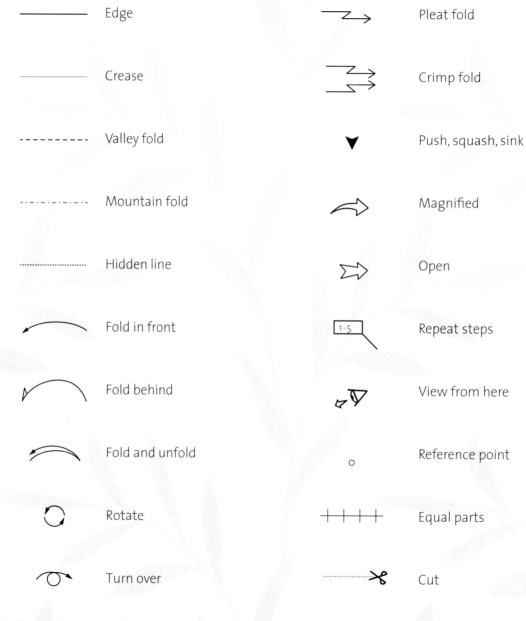	Pleat fold
————	Crease		Crimp fold
- - - - - -	Valley fold		Push, squash, sink
-·-·-·-·-	Mountain fold		Magnified
··············	Hidden line		Open
	Fold in front		Repeat steps
	Fold behind		View from here
	Fold and unfold		Reference point
	Rotate		Equal parts
	Turn over		Cut

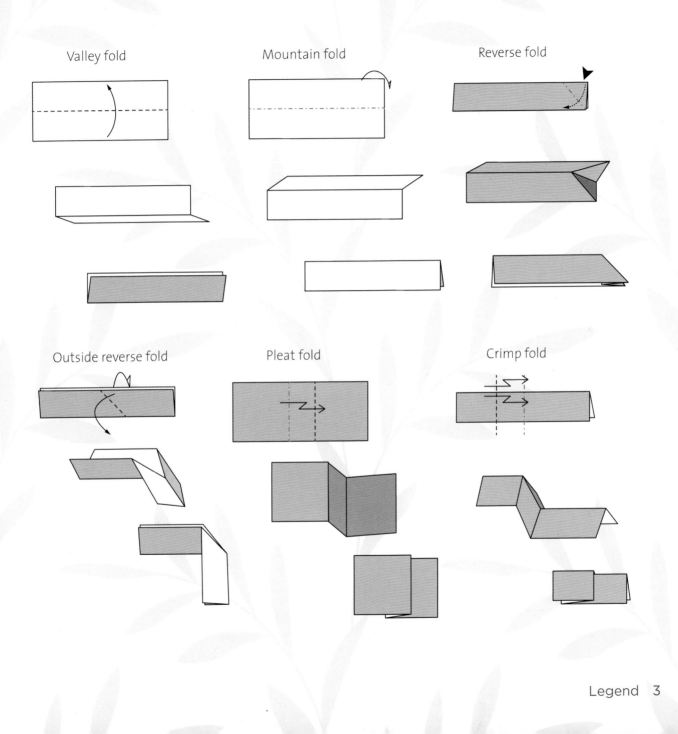

Valley fold

Mountain fold

Reverse fold

Outside reverse fold

Pleat fold

Crimp fold

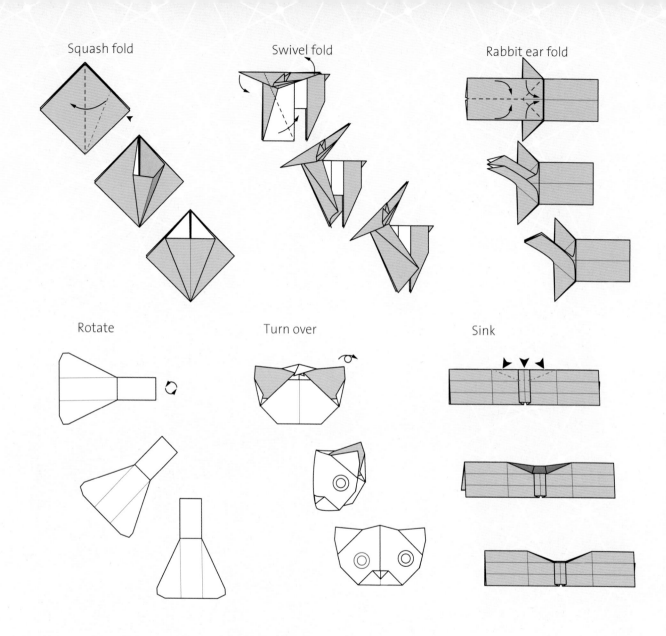

Squash fold

Swivel fold

Rabbit ear fold

Rotate

Turn over

Sink

Cutting Paper to a Dollar Bill-Sized Ratio

1

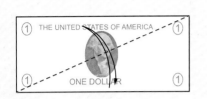

Fold a dollar bill diagonally. Crease well. Unfold.

2

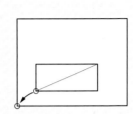

Position the corner of the dollar bill with the corner of the paper you want to use. Make sure the edges are also aligned.

3

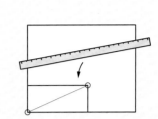

Place a ruler aligned with the diagonal of the dollar bill and all the way from the corner to the opposite edge.

4

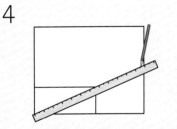

Use a pencil to mark by the edge.

5

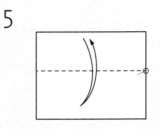

Fold at the mark, parallel to the edges. Unfold.

6

Cut along the crease line. Keep the bottom piece.

7

Dollar bill-sized paper completed.

SIMPLE MODELS

$2 Square

With this method of locking two one-dollar bills together, you can now fold all of your favorite origami models that start with a square.

1

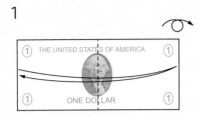

Start with George side up. Mountain fold in half. Unfold. Turn over.

2

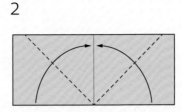

Fold the edges to the vertical line just created, on both left and right.

3

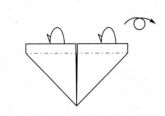

Mountain fold over the edges. Turn over.

4

(x 2)

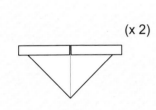

Repeat the steps to fold a second identical unit. Align the units as indicated on the next step.

5

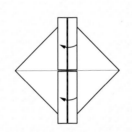

Unfold the flaps on one of the units.

6

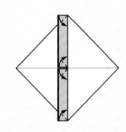

Fold the corners, edge to the edge.

7

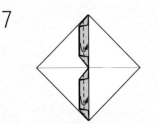

Valley fold the edge to the edge.

8

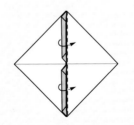

Tuck the flaps inside the pocket.

9

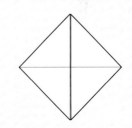

Square completed.

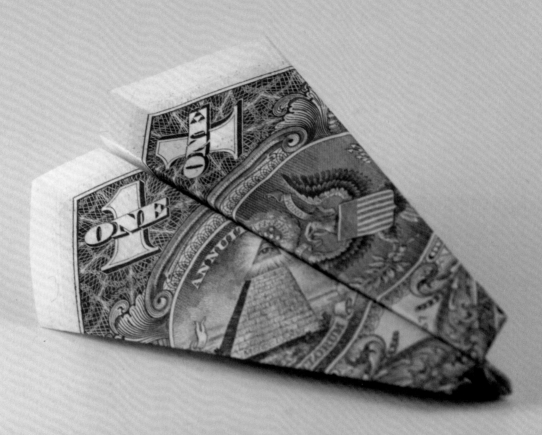

Airplane

Watch your money fly away with this model.

1

Start with George side up. Fold in half. Unfold.

2

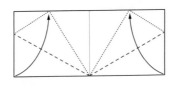

Fold the corner to the edge.

3

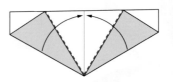

Fold the edge to the center line.

4

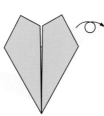

Turn over.

5

Fold the edge to the center line. Unfold.

6

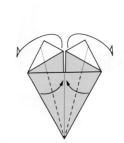

Valley fold the top layer, allowing the flap on the back to flip out.

7

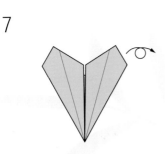

Turn over.

8

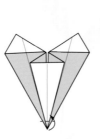

Fold the tip just a little bit. Note: there are no precise references.

9

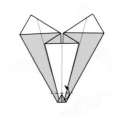

Fold once again.

10

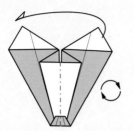

Mountain fold in half. Rotate.

11

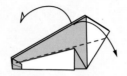

Open the wings using the existing creases.

12

Airplane completed.

Fun fact: The paper airplane was invented by Takuo Toda, who also holds the record for the longest indoor flight of an origami plane—22.48 seconds.

Box 1

This simple box, based on the traditional "magazine box," is perfect for storing spare change and other small objects.

1

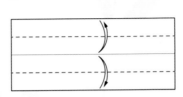

Start with George side up. Fold in half. Unfold.

2

Fold the edge to the center. Unfold.

3

Fold in half. Unfold.

4

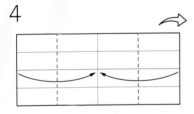

Fold the edges to the center.

5

Fold the corner to the line.

6

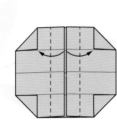

Fold the edge to the edges.

7

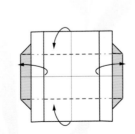

Fold wrapping over the edges.

8

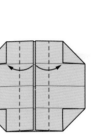

Open the edges, making the model three-dimensional.

9

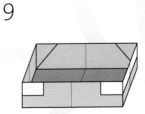

Box completed.

Box 1   15

Box 2

This variation of the traditional "magazine box" will fit all of your slightly larger items that do not fit in the previous box. It will also fit Box 1!

1

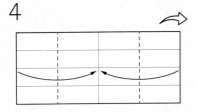

Start with George side up. Fold in half. Unfold.

2

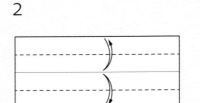

Fold the edge to the center. Unfold.

3

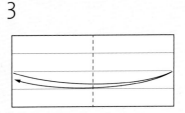

Fold in half. Unfold.

4

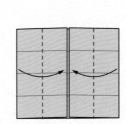

Fold the edges to the center.

5

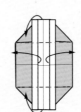

Fold the edges to the center.

6

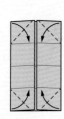

Fold the corners to the line.

7

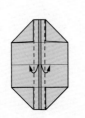

Fold wrapping over the edges.

8

Open the edges, making the model three-dimensional.

9

Box completed.

Box 2   17

Cat Head

My cat Domino would never let me live it down if I didn't include a cat model. He sat on me and supervised the making of this book, only occasionally demanding that I pet him instead.

1

Start with green "ONE" side up. Fold the edge to the letter ONE.

2

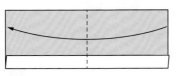

Fold in half, edge to edge.

3

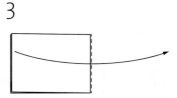

Unfold.

4

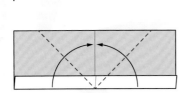

Fold the edge to the vertical line just created, on both left and right.

5

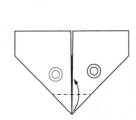

There are no real references so you can use your judgment to fold about the point indicated.

6

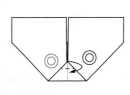

Fold the tip down, to shape the nose.

7

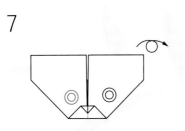

Turn over.

8

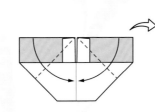

Fold the edges to the vertical line.

9

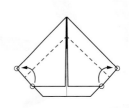

Fold the flaps diagonally, corner to corner.

10

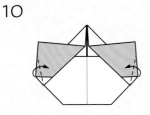

Fold the corners as indicated. There are no reference points for this step.

11

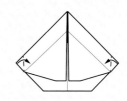

Unfold the flaps.

12

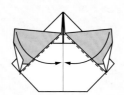

Fold the corners.

13

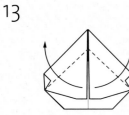

Fold using the existing creases.

14

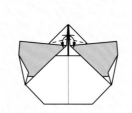

Fold the corners down. No reference points.

15

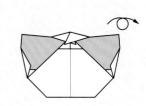

Turn over.

16

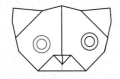

Cat Head completed.

Fun fact: The word "origami" originates from two Japanese words, "ori" (folded) and "kami" (paper). The Japanese written word "kami" is the same word used for spirit or god, and certain religious ceremonies feature origami models.

Erlenmeyer Flask

The Erlenmeyer flask was named after the chemist Emil Erlenmeyer, who created it in 1860.

1

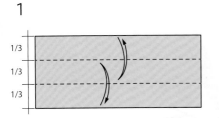

Start with "green" side up. Fold in thirds. Unfold.

2

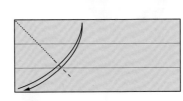

Fold the edge to the edge and pinch on the crease. Unfold.

3

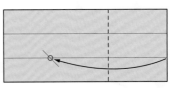

Fold the edge to the intersection indicated.

4

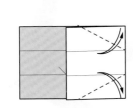

Valley fold, as indicated. Unfold.

5

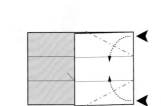

Reverse fold, using the creases created on the previous step.

6

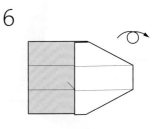

Turn over.

7

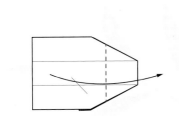

Valley fold.

8

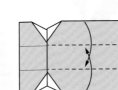

Valley fold, using the existing creases.

9

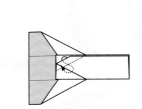

Fold the edge inside the pocket, locking it in place.

10

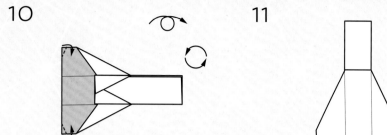

Fold the corners. Turn over.
Rotate.

11

Erlenmeyer Flask completed.

Fun fact: The United States one-dollar bill is the most common denomination of American currency. It makes up about 45 percent of all bills, and there are eleven billion one-dollar bills in circulation.

Fish

This model was inspired by the traditional model "twisted fish."

1

Start with George side up.
Mountain fold in half. Unfold.

2

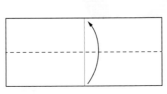

Fold in half.

3

Fold the edge to the center line.

4

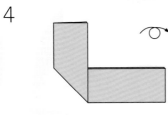

Turn over.

5

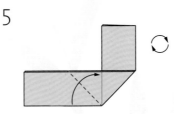

Fold the edge to the center line.
Rotate.

6

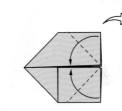

Fold the edges to the edge.

7

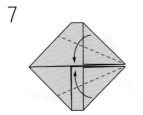

Fold the edges to the edge.

8

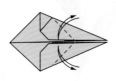

Valley fold the top flap
downward. Crease well. Unfold.
Valley fold the bottom flap
upward. Crease well. Unfold.

9

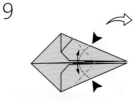

Reverse fold using the creases
created on the previous step.
Arrange the flaps so that the one
coming from the top stays on top.

10

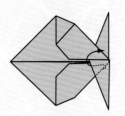

Rearrange the tail flaps to lock the model.

11

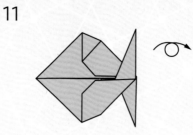

Turn over.

12

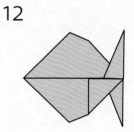

Fish completed.

Fun fact: The dollar bill measures 2.61 inches wide by 6.14 inches long, with a thickness of 0.0043 inches.

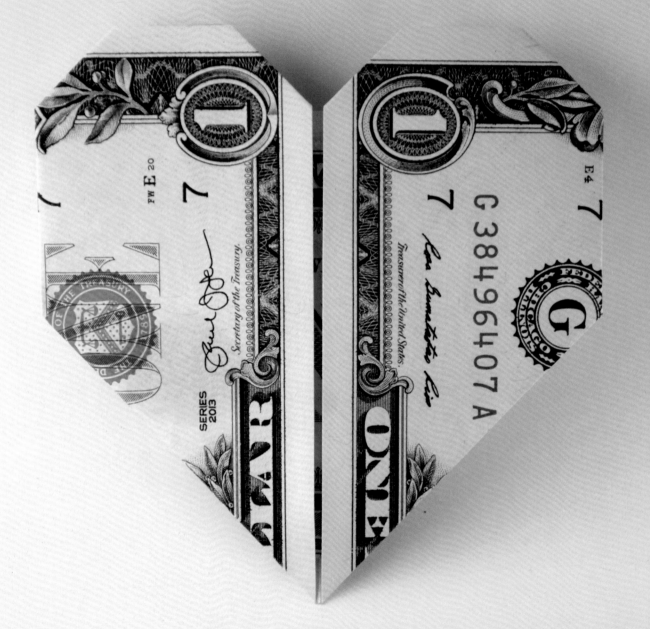

Heart

A heart that is simple and fun to fold for beginners and experts alike. Once folded, you'll want to give this money to your honey!

1

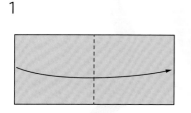

Start with the green side up.
Fold in half.

2

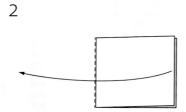

Unfold.

3

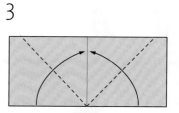

Fold the edge to the vertical line.

4

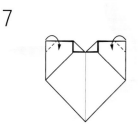

Turn over.

5

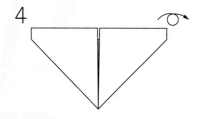

Fold the edge to the edge.

6

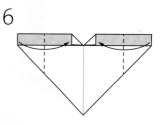

Fold the edge to the edge.

7

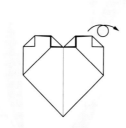

Fold the corners.

8

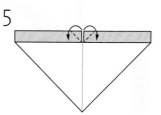

Turn over.

9

Heart completed.

Lily

Based on a traditional model, this has been adapted to be folded out of dollars using the $2 Square (page 9).

1

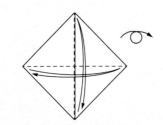

Start with a $2 square. Fold the diagonals. Unfold. Turn over.

2

Fold in half. Unfold.

3

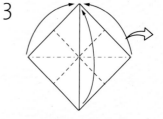

Fold all the corners together.

4

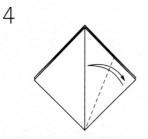

Fold the edge to the center. Unfold.

5

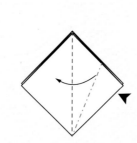

Open and squash fold.

6

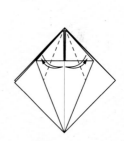

Fold the edge to the center. Unfold.

7

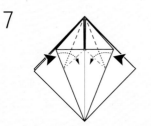

Reverse fold, as indicated.

8

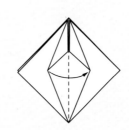

Valley fold.

9

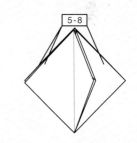

Repeat steps 5 to 8 on the other remaining three flaps.

10

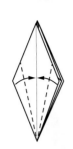

Fold the edge to the center.

11

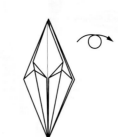

Turn over.

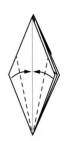

12

Fold the edge to the center.

13

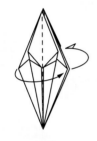

Fold the top two left flaps to the right, and the bottom two right flaps to the left.

14

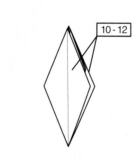

10 - 12

Repeat steps 10 to 12 in front and on the back.

15

Curl the petals, make the model three-dimensional.

16

Lily completed.

Fun fact: One would need to fold a dollar bill about 4,000 double folds, first backward and then forward, before it will tear!

Pizza Slice

You can fold your pizza and eat it, too.

1

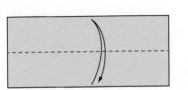

Start with the green side up.
Fold in half. Unfold.

2

 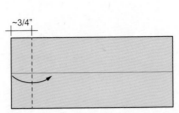

Fold about a ¾ inch.

3

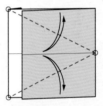

Mountain fold backward,
using the edge on the top as
reference.

4

 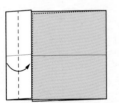

Fold the edge to edge.

5

 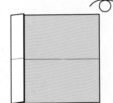

Turn over.

6

Fold between the points
indicated. Crease well. Unfold.

7

Fold the edge to the crease line.

8

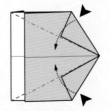

Reverse fold so that the
triangular flap will become
hidden between the layers.

9

 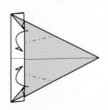

Mountain fold between the
layers. No precise reference
points.

10

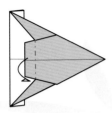

Mountain fold inside the pocket, locking the flap.

11

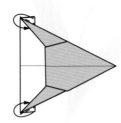

Wrap around the corners along the edge.

12

Turn over.

13

Pizza Slice completed.

Fun fact: The dollar bill isn't made out of paper; it's actually made out of cotton and linen!

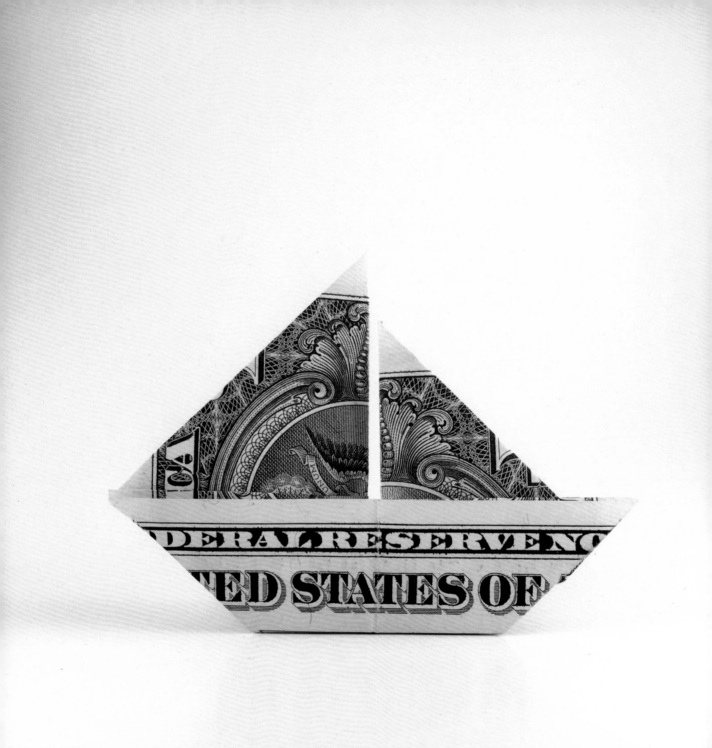

Sailboat

This model is based on the traditional sailboat origami model.

1

Start with George side up. Fold in half. Unfold.

2

Mountain fold in half.

3

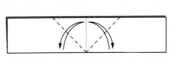

Fold the edge to the center line. Unfold.

4

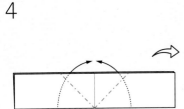

Reverse fold.

5

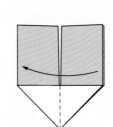

Valley fold the top layer.

6

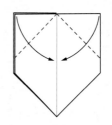

Valley fold the edge to the center.

7

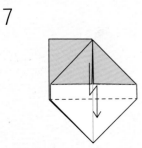

Pleat fold.

8

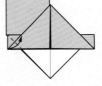

Fold the corner.

9

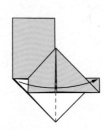

Valley fold.

10

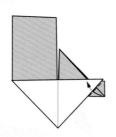

Fold the corner between the layers, creating a lock.

11

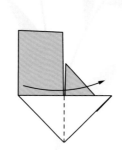

Valley fold the top layer.

12

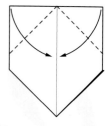

Valley fold the edge to the center.

13

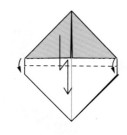

Pleat fold.

14

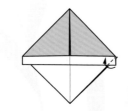

Valley fold the top layer.

15

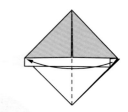

Valley fold.

16

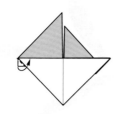

Fold the corner between the layers, creating a lock.

17

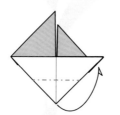

Mountain fold the corner to the back.

18

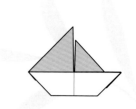

Sailboat completed.

Fun fact: Any laminar (flat) materials can be used to fold origami; the only requirement is that it should be able to hold a crease.

Simple Bird

A simple bird for those who are just starting out folding.

1

Start with George side up. Fold in half. Unfold.

2

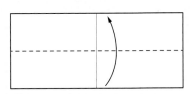

Fold in half.

3

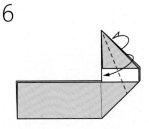

Fold the edge to the line. Unfold.

4

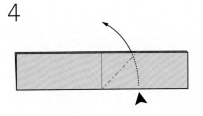

Reverse fold.

5

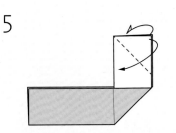

Fold edge to the edge in front and on the back.

6

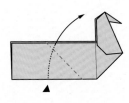

Fold edge to the edge in front and on the back.

7

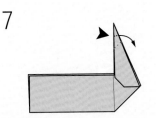

Reverse fold.

8

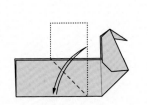

Fold as indicated. No reference points. Unfold.

9

Reverse fold.

10

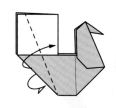

Fold edge to the edge in front and on the back.

11

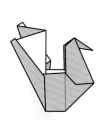

Open the flaps slightly to the side, creating a volume to the tail.

12

Simple Bird completed.

Fun fact: The smallest origami crane in the world measures 0.1 by 0.1 mm. It was folded by 82-year-old Naito Akira, who used a microscope and folding plastic film.

Tulip

A traditional tulip. Now, you can fold it out of dollar bills by first making the $2 Square (page 9).

1

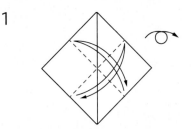

Start with a $2 square. Fold in half. Unfold. Turn over.

2

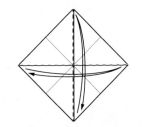

Fold the diagonals. Unfold.

3

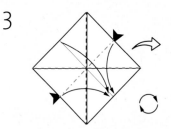

Fold edge to edge, incorporating the reverse folds. Rotate.

4

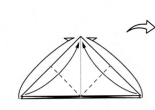

Fold the corner to corner.

5

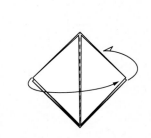

Fold the top left flap to the right and the bottom right flap to the left.

6

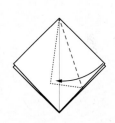

Pivoting from the top, fold the corner past the center line, as indicated.

7

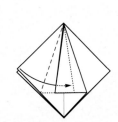

Pivoting from the top, fold the corner inside the pocket of the previous flap, as indicated. This should lock the flaps together.

8

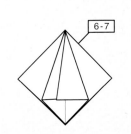

Repeat steps 6 to 7 on the back.

9

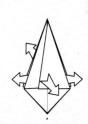

Find the opening at the bottom, in the center. Carefully blow it up, making the model three-dimensional.

10

Curl the petals.

11

Tulip completed.

INTERMEDIATE MODELS

Bow

This was one of the first models I designed. At the time, I was working at a small gift shop that provided gift wrapping services. After making hundreds of ribbon bows, I wanted to create a a bow made out of dollar bills. This model is dedicated to my wonderful bosses Sue and Kris Roberts.

1

Start with George side up.
Fold in half. Unfold.

2

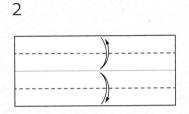

Fold the edge to the center.
Unfold.

3

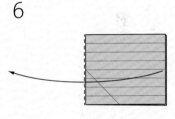

Fold and unfold into eights.

4

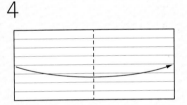

Fold in half.

5

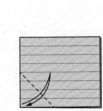

Fold the edge to the line.
Unfold.

6

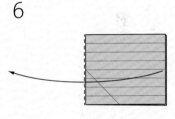

Unfold.

7

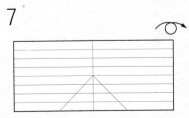

Turn over.

8

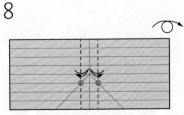

Fold and unfold through the intersection point indicated.
Turn over.

9

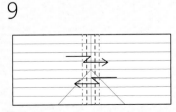

Pleat fold.

10

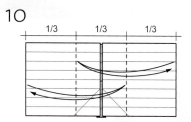

Fold in thirds. Unfold.

11

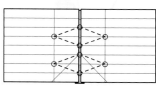

Create valley fold creases as indicated.

12

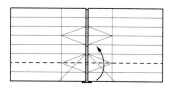

Fold using the existing crease.

13

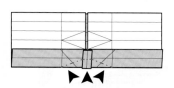

Push inside and sink, and squash the paper inside to make it flat.

14

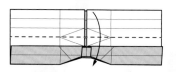

Fold using the existing crease.

15

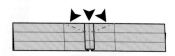

Push inside and sink, and squash the paper inside to make it flat, similar to step 13.

16

Fold using the existing crease.

17

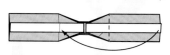

Fold using the existing crease. You may want to repeat the next few steps on both sides, if it is easier, and don't mind the overlapping flaps.

18

Fold the corner up. There are no precise references, but somewhere around the middle of the edge, to the lower right corner.

19

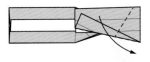

There are no precise references. Valley fold the flap on an angle.

20

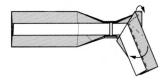

Swivel fold, narrowing the flap.

21

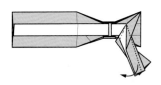

Swivel the layer slightly.

22

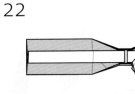

Create the split by valley folding from the corners and squashing the middle.

23

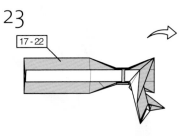

17 - 22

Repeat steps 17 to 22 on the other side.

24

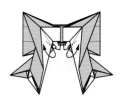

Pull out trapped paper.

25

Mountain fold, to create a small lock.

26

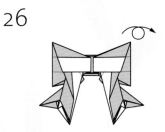

Turn over.

27

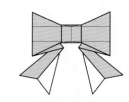

Bow completed.

Bow Tie

If you ever find yourself in need of an emergency bow tie, look no further—all you'll need is a dollar from your wallet.

1

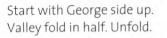

Start with George side up. Valley fold in half. Unfold.

2

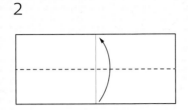

Fold in half.

3

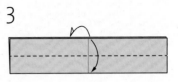

Fold the edge to the edge in front and on the back.

4

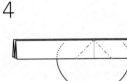

Mountain fold diagonally.

5

Fold the diagonal, edge to edge. Crease well. Unfold.

6

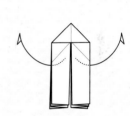

Unfold.

7

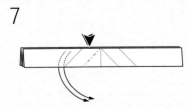

Open the model slightly and double reverse fold.

8

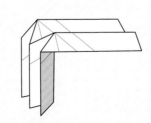

In progress . . .

9

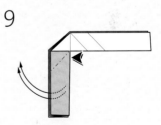

Open the model slightly and double reverse fold.

10

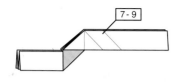

Repeat steps 7 to 9 on the other side.

11

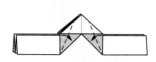

Fold edge to edge.

12

Fold corner to corner.

13

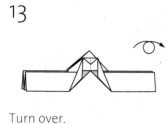

Turn over.

14

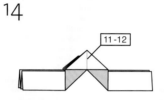

Repeat steps 11 to 12 on the other side.

15

Fold the top layer up.

16

Fold corner to corner.

17

Release the paper trapped between the layers, squash to make it flat.

18

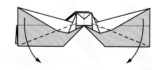

Fold the corner down, as far as it goes.

19

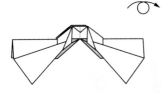

Turn over.

20

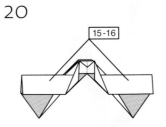

Repeat steps 15 to 16.

21

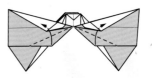

Fold the corner under the layer.

22

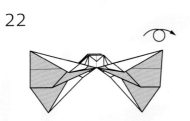

Turn over.

23

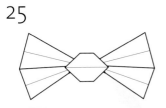

Valley fold, opening the center.

24

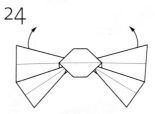

Pivot to align the bow.

25

Bow Tie completed.

Bulldog

This was one of the first models I designed, as well as one of my current favorites.

1

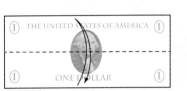

Start with George side up, as indicated. Fold in half. Unfold.

2

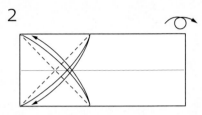

Fold the diagonals. Unfold. Turn over.

3

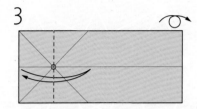

Fold between at the intersection point indicated. Unfold. Turn over.

4

Fold the edge to the line. Crease all the way. Unfold.

5

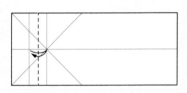

Fold the line to the line. Crease all the way. Unfold.

6

Fold the line to the line. Pinch in the center. Unfold.

7

Fold the edge to the pinch mark created on the last step.

8

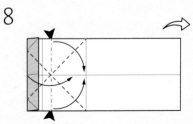

Collapse the water-bomb base.

9

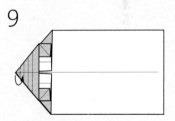

Fold the corner to the intersection point.

10

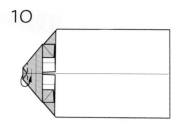

Fold the edge to the pinch mark.

11

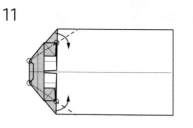

Valley fold the lower layer only, between the reference points indicated.

12

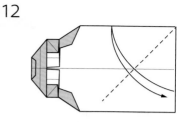

Fold edge to the edge. Crease as indicated. Unfold.

13

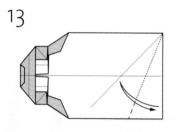

Fold edge to the line. Pinch by the edge. Unfold.

14

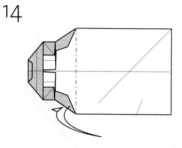

Mountain fold corner to corner. Unfold.

15

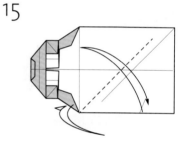

Fold edge to the line. Crease as indicated. Unfold.

16

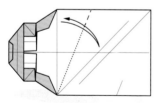

Fold line to the line. Pinch by the edge. Unfold.

17

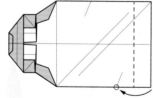

Fold the corner to the pinch mark.

18

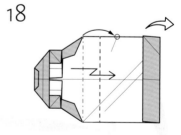

Pleat fold. Fold the mountain edge to the pinch mark.

19

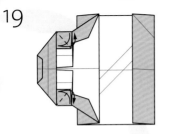

Fold and unfold, on the existing crease.

20

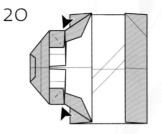

Reverse fold.

21

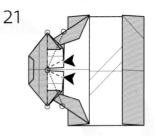

Reverse fold as indicated, leaving the ear flaps sticking out.

22

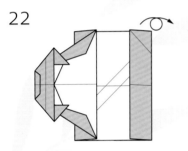

Turn over.

23

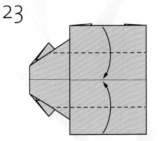

Fold the edges to the center.

24

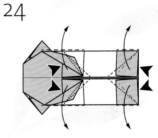

Valley fold and squash the top layer, creating new flaps.

25

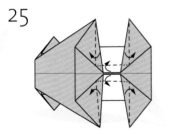

Valley fold, aligned to the edges of the flaps. Create a small squash by the corners.

26

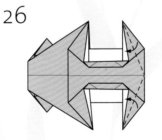

Valley fold.

27

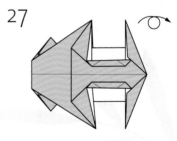

Turn over.

28

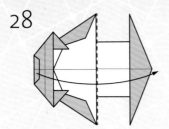

Fold the entire flap on its hinge.

29

Valley fold.

30

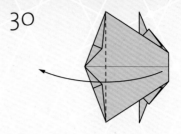

Fold the flap back on its hinge.

31

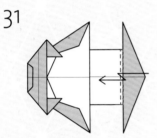

Create a narrow pleat.

32

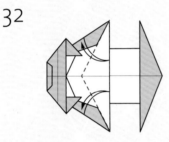

Fold the edge to the edge. Unfold.

33

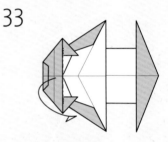

Mountain fold the head.

34

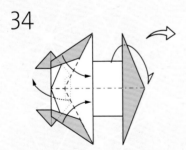

Mountain fold the model in half, allowing the head to pivot. Note: keep the head rounded for three-dimensional finish.

35

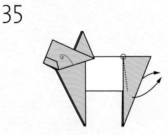

Swivel the back legs.

36

Mountain fold the ears.

37

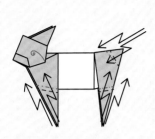

Pleat the legs. Crimp the tail.

38

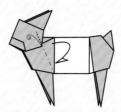

Mountain fold in front and on the back.

39

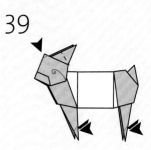

Reverse fold the feet. Reverse fold the head.

40

Bulldog completed.

Capricorn

Capricorn, with the upper body of a mountain goat and the lower body of a fish, is the tenth astrological zodiac sign.

1

Start with George side up. Fold in half. Unfold.

2

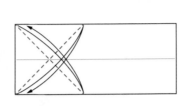

Fold the diagonals. Unfold.

3

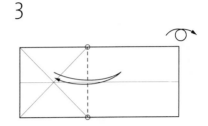

Fold between the points indicated. Turn over.

4

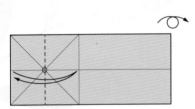

Fold edge to the line at the intersection point. Unfold. Turn over.

5

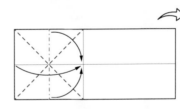

Collapse the water-bomb base.

6

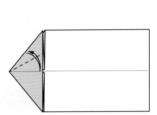

Fold edge to the line. Unfold.

7

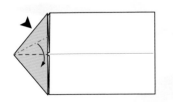

Open and squash fold.

8

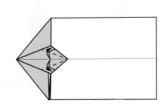

Fold edge to the line. Unfold.

9

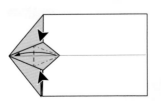

Petal fold.

10

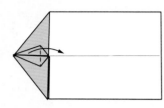

Valley fold.

11

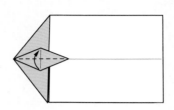

Valley fold.

12

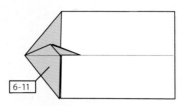

Repeat steps 6 to 11 on the other side.

13

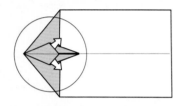

Pull out paper.

14

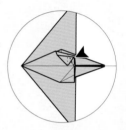

Fold the corner to the center line.

15

Push the corner, creasing a small asymmetric reverse fold.

16

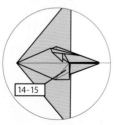

Repeat steps 14 to 15 on the other side.

17

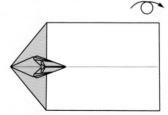

Turn over.

18

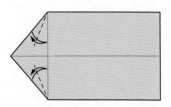

Fold the edge to the line. Crease as indicated. Unfold.

19

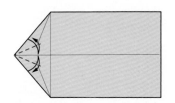

Fold the edge to the line. Crease as indicated. Unfold.

20

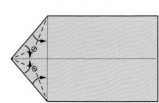

Reinforce the creases, in preparation for the squash. The model will not lie flat.

21

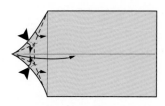

Fold the flap to the opposite side, and squash to make it flat. See next step for expected result.

22

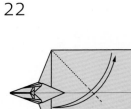

Fold the edge to edge. Pinch on the center line. Unfold.

23

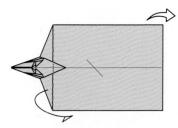

Mountain fold by the edge using the existing crease.

24

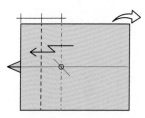

Mountain fold at the intersection point, and pleat fold to the edge.

25

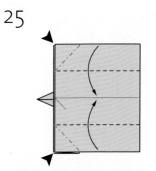

Valley fold the edge to the center, squashing the corners to make it flat.

26

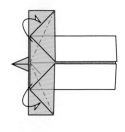

Mountain fold the corners so that they are hidden inside.

27

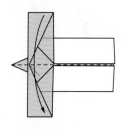

Fold the entire model in half.

28

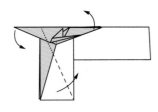

Swivel fold.

29

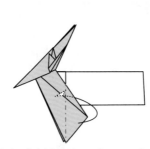

Mountain fold by the edge, and tuck inside in front and on the back.

30

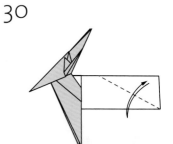

Fold and unfold, as indicated.

31

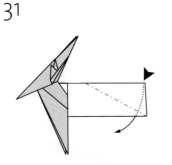

Reverse fold, using the creases created on the previous step.

32

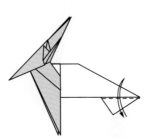

Fold and unfold, as indicated.

33

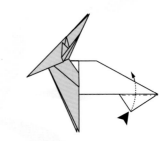

Reverse fold.

34

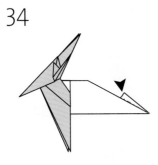

Reverse fold.

35

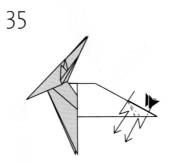

Squash and flatten with a small pleat in front and on the back.

36

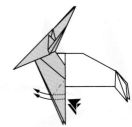

Reverse fold in front and on the back.

37

Reverse fold.

38

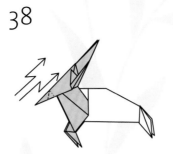

Crimp fold to create the beard.

39

Narrow and curl the horns.

40

Capricorn completed.

Crane

This is a traditional crane, perhaps the most iconic origami model. It has been adapted to be folded out of dollar bills using the $2 Square (page 9).

1

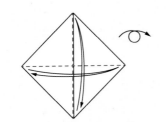

Start with a $2 square. Fold the diagonals. Unfold. Turn over.

2

Fold in half. Unfold.

3

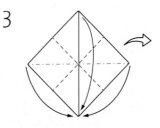

Fold all the corners together.

4

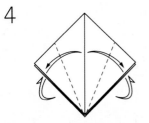

Fold the edge to the center, in front on the back. Unfold.

5

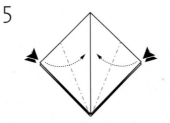

Reverse fold all the corners using the creases created on the previous step.

6

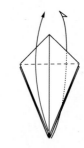

Fold the triangular flap up, in front and on the back.

7

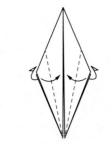

Fold the edge to the center, in front and on the back.

8

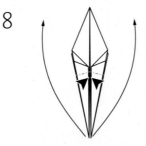

Reverse fold.

9

Reverse fold.

10

Spread the wings and open the body.

11

Crane completed.

Fun fact: According to an ancient Japanese legend, if you fold 1,000 cranes you will be granted a wish. In 1955, Sadako Sasaki, a twelve-year-old girl who was exposed to radiation from the Hiroshima atomic bombs during World War II, brought public awareness to this myth when she embarked on a mission to fold 1,000 cranes. Unfortunately, she only folded 644 cranes before passing away, and her friends and family completed the rest of the cranes.

Goat

Goats are members of the bovidae family and are closely related to sheep. In some places, you can rent a goat to keep your lawn in check!

1

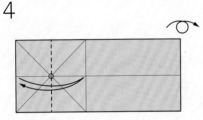

Start with George side up, as indicated. Fold in half. Unfold.

2

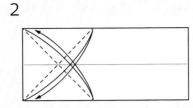

Fold the diagonals. Unfold.

3

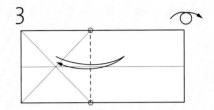

Fold between the points indicated. Turn over.

4

Fold edge to the line at the intersection point. Unfold. Turn over.

5

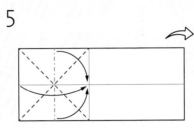

Collapse the water-bomb base.

6

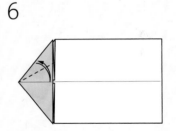

Fold edge to the line. Unfold.

7

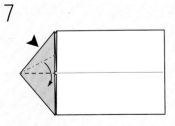

Open and squash fold.

8

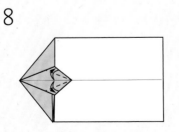

Fold edge to the line. Unfold.

9

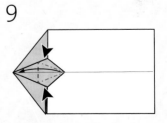

Petal fold.

10

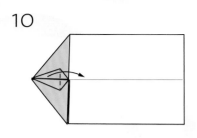

Valley fold.

11

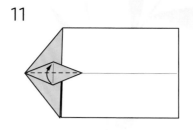

Valley fold.

12

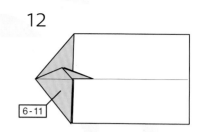

Repeat steps 6 to 11 on the other side.

13

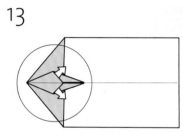

Pull out paper.

14

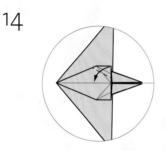

Fold the corner to the center line.

15

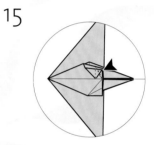

Push the corner, creasing a small asymmetric reverse fold.

16

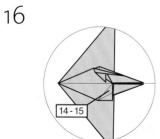

Repeat steps 14 to 15 on the other side.

17

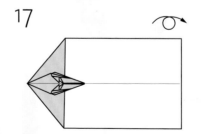

Turn over.

18

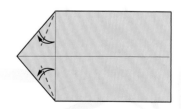

Fold the edge to the line. Crease as indicated. Unfold.

19

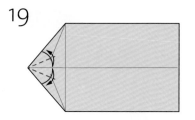

Fold the edge to the line. Crease as indicated. Unfold.

20

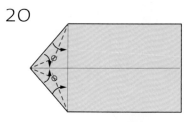

Reinforce the creases, in preparation for the squash. The model will not lie flat.

21

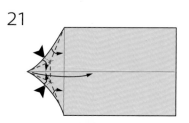

Fold the flap to the opposite side and squash to make it flat. See next step for expected result.

22

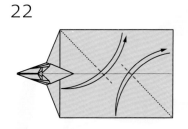

Fold the edge to edge. Pinch on the center line. Unfold.

23

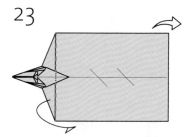

Mountain fold by the edge using the existing crease.

24

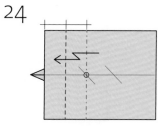

Mountain fold at the intersection point and pleat fold to the edge.

25

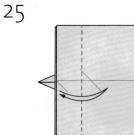

Valley fold the top layer only, aligning to the edge underneath. Unfold.

26

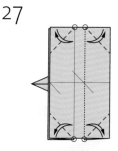

Mountain fold to the intersection point.

27

Fold edge to the edge underneath. On the left, fold the top two layers of paper only. Unfold.

28

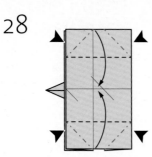

Squash the corners and fold the edge to the center line.

29

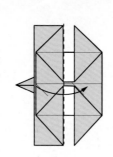

Fold the top flap to the right.

30

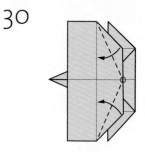

Valley fold, from the corner to the center.

31

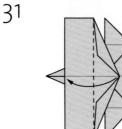

Fold the flap back to the left.

32

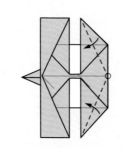

Valley fold, from the corner to the center.

33

Crimp.

34

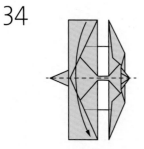

Fold the entire model in half.

35

Swivel.

36

Mountain fold by the edge. Tuck inside in front and on the back.

37

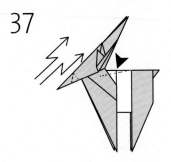

Crimp to create the beard. Sink the back.

38

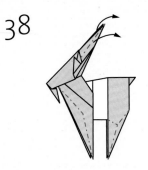

Shape the model: narrow and curl the horns, narrow the legs, optionally add reverse folds for the legs.

39

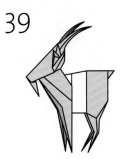

Goat completed.

Manatee

Manatees are also known as sea cows. If you pay close attention to the Manatee, Seal (page 105), and Walrus (page 121) models in this book, you'll notice that they are folded in similar fashions to each other.

1

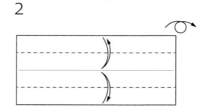

Start with George side up. Fold in half. Unfold.

2

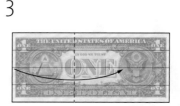

Fold the edge to the center. Unfold. Turn over.

3

Fold using the printed pattern as reference.

4

Fold the edge to the line. Crease as indicated. Unfold.

5

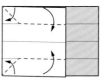

Reinforce the creases in preparation for the squash. The model will not lie flat.

6

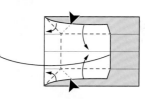

Fold the flap to the opposite side and squash to make it flat. See next step for expected result.

7

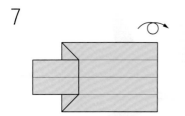

Turn over.

8

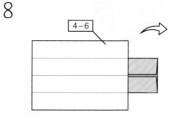

Repeat steps 4 to 6 on the other side.

9

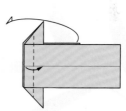

Fold the edges, allowing the flap to flip out. There is some paper on the back that will not lie flat.

10

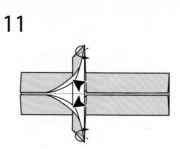

Turn over.

11

Swivel some paper by the corner and squash to make the model flat.

12

Fold in half.

13

Crimp fold.

14

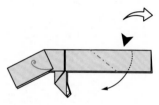

Fold and unfold all layers to pre-crease.

15

Reverse fold.

16

Fold and unfold to pre-crease.

17

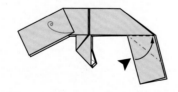

Open and squash fold.

18

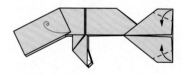

Mountain fold the corners inside the layers.

19

Fold edge to edge. Crease well. Unfold.

20

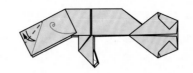

Fold edge to line. Crease well. Unfold.

21

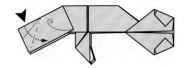

Reverse fold.

22

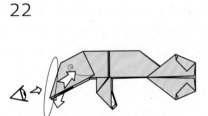

Open slightly and view inside the reverse fold.

23

Using the pre-crease lines, fold the edge to the center. Note: the head should not be round.

24

Fold the corners inside the head, wrapping along the edges underneath.

25

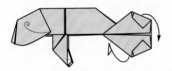

Flip the tail to make it perpendicular to the body. Shape the body to become three-dimensional.

26

Manatee completed.

Manta Ray

A beautiful creature of the sea. Some popular tourist destinations feature sites where manta rays congregate and feed.

1

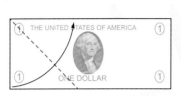

Start with George side up. Fold edge to edge.

2

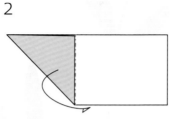

Mountain fold along the edge.

3

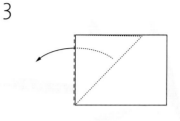

Unfold everything.

4

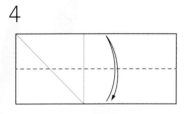

Fold in half. Unfold.

5

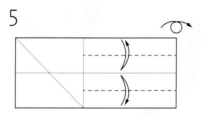

Fold edge to the line. Crease well. Unfold. Turn over.

6

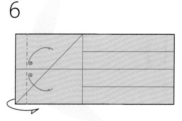

Mountain fold, leaving a tiny bit of space near the eye swirls.

7

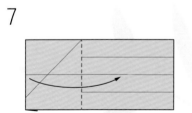

Fold using the existing crease.

8

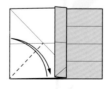

Fold the raw edge to the folded edge on the top layer only. Crease where indicated. Unfold.

9

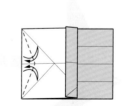

Fold the folded edge to the line, allowing the long flap to flip out. Crease where indicated. Unfold.

10

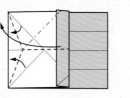

Rabbit ear fold.

11

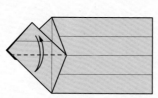

Fold and unfold on its "hinge."

12

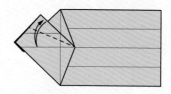

Fold the edge to the center line. Crease well. Unfold.

13

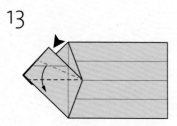

Open and squash.

14

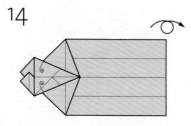

Turn over.

15

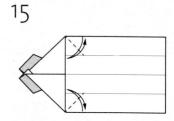

Fold the edge to the edge. Unfold.

16

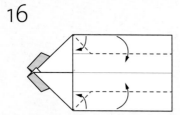

Reinforce the creases, in preparation for the squash. The model will not lie flat.

17

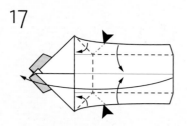

Fold the flap to the opposite side and squash to make it flat. See next step for expected result.

18

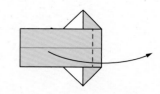

Fold the flap. There is some paper that will not lie flat.

19

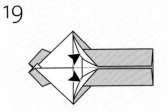

Squash fold to make the model flat.

20

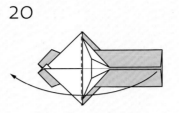

Fold the flap on its "hinge."

21

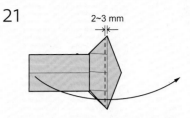

Fold 2 or 3 millimeters from the line, creating a new crease.

22

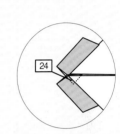

Detailed view next.

23

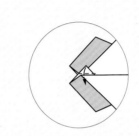

Fold the corner under the top layer.

24

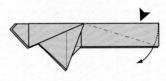

Fold the other corner under the top layer, making the distribution symmetrical.

25

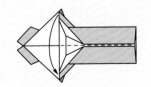

Fold in half.

26

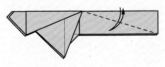

Fold corner to corner. Crease well. Unfold.

27

Reverse fold.

28

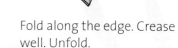

Fold along the edge. Crease well. Unfold.

29

Reverse fold.

30

Fold along the edge. Crease well. Unfold.

31

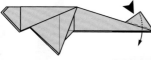

Reverse fold.

32

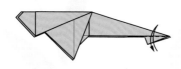

Fold along the edge. Crease well. Unfold.

33

Fold the flap below the first layer, creating a lock.

34

Open. Note: the model will be concave and not flat.

35

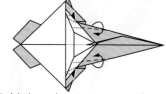

Fold the edge, to narrow the tail. Create a small squash under the paper to make it flat.

36

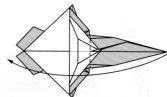

Fold the tail at the vertex, making the model lie completely flat.

37

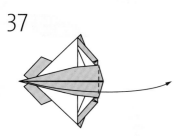

Fold the tail corner to corner, maintaining the model flat.

38

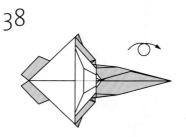

Turn over.

39

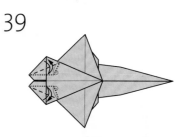

Fold and unfold.

40

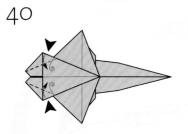

Reverse fold.

41

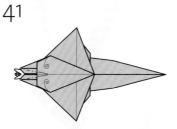

Mountain fold the flaps, in preparation to split the cephalic lobes.

42

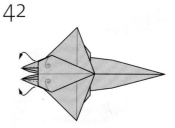

Pinch to narrow the cephalic lobes and shape it by making it round.

43

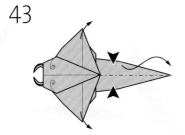

Mountain fold the tail to narrow it; shape with curves. Slightly curl the "wings."

44

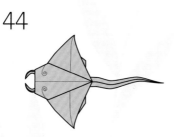

Manta Ray completed.

Norman the Duck

I have a pet duck named Norman. He loves to nibble at my toes and run in circles around me.

1

Start with George side up, as indicated. Fold in half. Unfold.

2

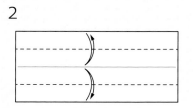

Fold in quarters. Unfold.

3

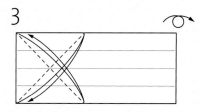

Fold the diagonals on the left side. Unfold. Turn over.

4

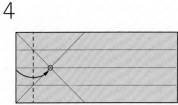

Fold edge to the intersection indicated.

5

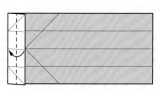

Fold edge to edge.

6

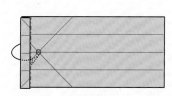

Fold along the edge, bringing behind the edges to the intersection.

7

Unfold. Turn over.

8

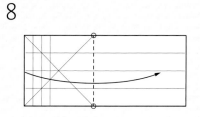

Fold between the points indicated.

9

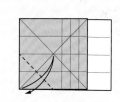

Fold the angle bisector, edge to the center line. Unfold.

10

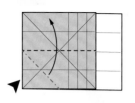

Open and squash fold.

11

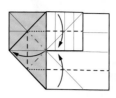

Collapse what looks like a petal fold.

12

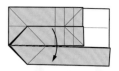

Fold the flap down.

13

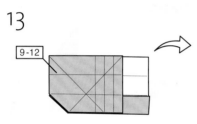

9-12

Repeat steps 9 to 12 on the other side.

14

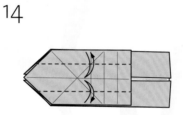

Fold edge to the center. Crease well. Unfold.

15

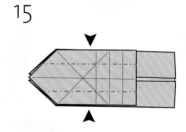

Open sink.

16

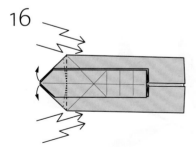

Crimp the flap to move the corners out, creating the tail feathers.

17

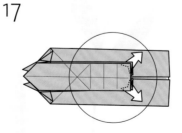

Stretch the layers. Detailed view next.

18

Using the existing creases, create an "Elias Stretch" fold.

19

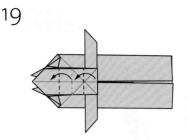

Fold over.

20

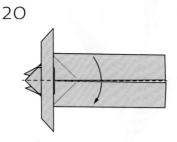

Fold in half.

21 (Reference points viewed from the top)

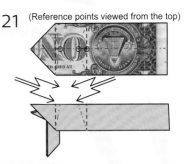

Crimp fold using the reference points indicated.

22

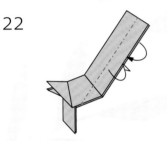

Fold the edge almost to the center. Leave a small gap of about 1 mm.

23

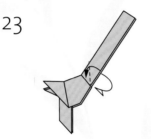

Outside reverse fold, edge to the edge.

24

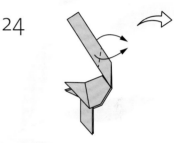

Outside reverse fold. No reference points. See next step for proportions expected.

25

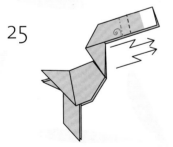

Crimp fold. The mountain fold should be right next to the eye swirls. And when the crimp is made, there should be only the white border showing where the beak is.

26

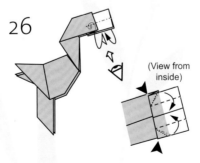

(View from inside)

Fold the edge inside, squashing the sides.

27

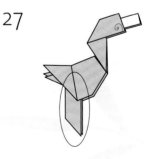

Details of the feet next.

28

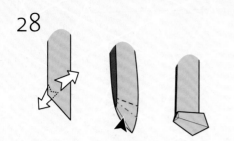

Opening the layers slightly, collapse the base to create a pentagonal shape.

29

For the final shaping, round the chest. Hold the neck and push down the beak down to create a triangular shape inside the head.

30

Duck completed.

Fun fact: In 1862, the first one-dollar bill was issued as a Legal Tender Note with a portrait of Salmon P. Chase, the Secretary of the Treasury. In 1869, the one-dollar bill was redesigned to feature a portrait of George Washington.

Rat

Not all rats are ugly, undesirable vermin. This dollar bill rat would make a great pet.

1

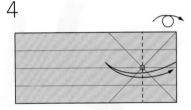

Start with George side up. Fold in half. Unfold.

2

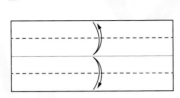

Fold the edge to the center. Unfold.

3

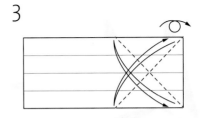

Fold the diagonal, edge to the edge. Unfold. Turn over.

4

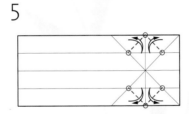

Fold at the intersection point. Unfold.

5

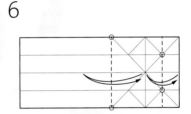

Fold the diagonals, between the reference points indicated. Unfold.

6

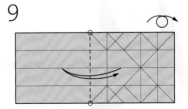

Fold between the reference points indicated. Unfold.

7

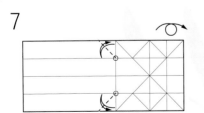

Fold the diagonal, starting from the intersection point indicated. Unfold. Turn over.

8

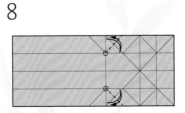

Fold the diagonal, starting from the intersection point indicated. Unfold.

9

Fold between the reference points indicated. Unfold. Turn over.

10

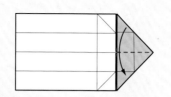

Using the existing creases, collapse what is known as the water-bomb base.

11

Valley fold the the triangular flap.

12

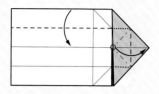

Using the existing creases, fold the point indicated to the corner, and flatten.

13

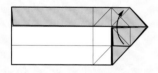

Valley fold the trapezoidal flap.

14

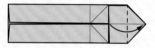

Repeat steps 11 to 13 on the other side.

15

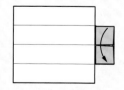

Valley fold the rectangular flap.

16

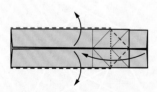

Open the long rectangular flaps, folding the whole unit from the right to the left.

17

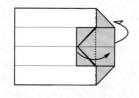

Mountain fold, allowing the whole unit to flip out.

18

Fold the top flap.

19

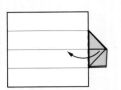

Valley fold the triangular flap.

20

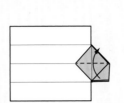

Fold the flap back to its original position.

21

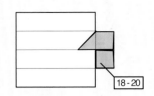

Repeat steps 18 to 20 on the other side.

22

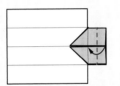

Fold the edge to the line.

23

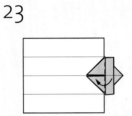

Valley fold.

24

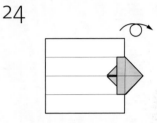

Turn over.

25

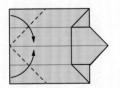

Fold the edge to the center.

26

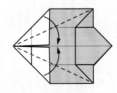

Fold corner to corner, edge towards the center, like an airplane fold.

27

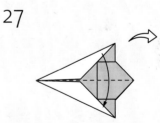

Fold in half.

28

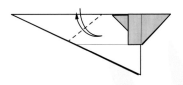

Fold the diagonal as indicated. There are no precise references. Unfold.

29

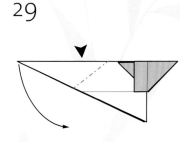

Reverse fold.

30

Fold edge to edge. Unfold.

31

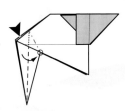

Reverse fold, connecting the point indicated with the previous crease.

32

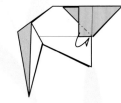

Mountain fold the corner under the layers, locking the head in place.

33

Pleat fold to create the front feet.

34

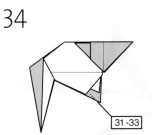

31-33

Repeat steps 31 to 33 on the other side.

35

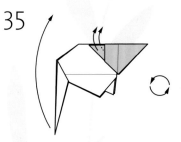

Fold the tail up, curl the ears. Rotate.

36

Rat completed.

Fun fact: The one-dollar bill is full of symbolisms featuring the number 13, if you can spot them! There are 13 stripes on the flag, 13 stars above the eagle, 13 steps on the pyramid, 13 leaves on the olive branch, 13 fruits, 13 arrows, and the two 13-letter mottos "E Pluribus Unum" on the ribbon in the eagle's beak and "Annuit Coeptis" above the pyramid. Some say that these symbols of 13 represent the 13 first states of independent America.

Seal

Leave one of these with your waiter or waitress at a restaurant to seal the deal.

1

Start with George side up. Mountain fold in half. Unfold.

2

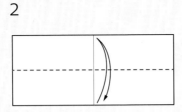

Fold in half. Unfold.

3

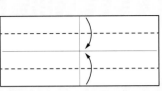

Fold the edge to the center.

4

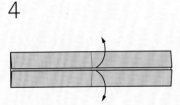

Unfold.

5

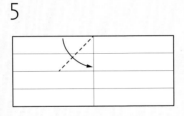

Fold the edge to line.

6

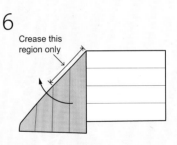

Crease only where indicated. Unfold.

7

Fold and unfold, similar to the last two steps.

8

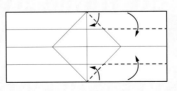

Reinforce the creases, in preparation for the squash. The model will not lie flat.

9

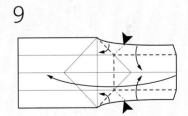

Fold the flap to the opposite side, and squash to make it flat. See next step for expected result.

10

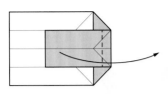

Fold the flap. There is some paper that will not lie flat.

11

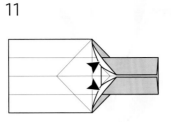

Squash fold to make the model flat.

12

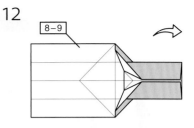

8–9

Repeat steps 8 to 9 on the other side.

13

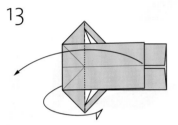

Mountain fold allowing the flap to flip out.

14

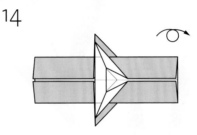

Turn over.

15

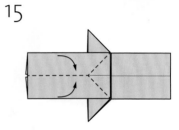

Rabbit ear fold, using the existing creases. The model will not lie flat.

16

Mountain fold in half. The model will be flat now.

17

Fold and unfold all layers to pre-crease.

18

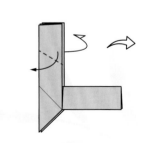

Outside reverse fold.

19

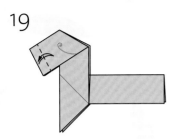

Fold and unfold to pre-crease.

20

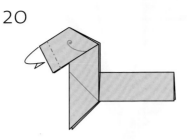

Mountain fold the edge between the layers.

21

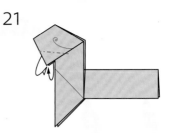

Mountain fold the corners inside the layers.

22

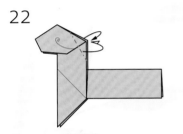

Mountain fold the corners inside the layers.

23

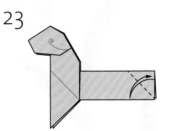

Fold the edge to edge. Unfold.

24

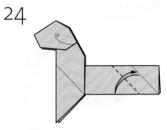

Fold and unfold.

25

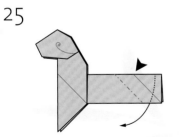

Reverse fold.

26

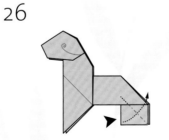

Reverse fold.

27

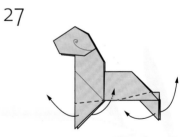

Open the fore-flippers and hind-flippers to make it stand.

28

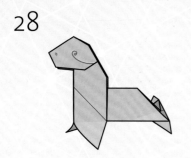

Seal completed.

Fun fact: There are many different types of origami in addition to dollar bill origami, which is also called moneygami. You can also fold action origami (origami that involves movement), modular origami (models that are put together from many identical pieces), and kirigami (a variation of origami that involves paper cutting).

Snake

A fun little model with a lot of character packed in.

1

Start with George side up. Fold in half. Unfold.

2

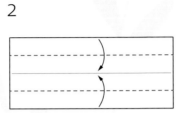

Fold the edge to the center.

3

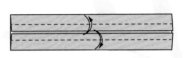

Fold the edge to slightly past the center line. Unfold.

4

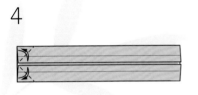

Fold the edge to the line. Unfold.

5

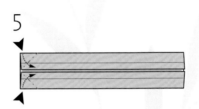

Reverse fold using the creases created on the previous step.

6

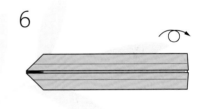

Turn over.

7

Mountain fold the corner inside.

8

Pleat fold.

9

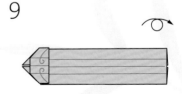

Turn over.

10

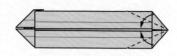

Fold edge to the center line.

11

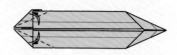

Fold edge to the center line.

12

Fold edge to the center line. Crease well. Unfold.

13

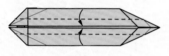

Fold using the existing creases.

14

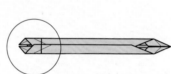

Detailed view next.

15

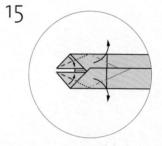

Using the existing creases, fold edge to the edge. Open the head slightly, squash to flatten.

16

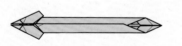

Turn over.

17

Shape the tongue.

18

Shape the body, making it narrower and curved.

19

Snake completed.

Fun fact: A typical lifespan of a one-dollar bill is 22 months.

Turkey

Gobble gobble! I designed this turkey right before Thanksgiving. Now this is one of my favorite designs to fold annually on turkey day.

1

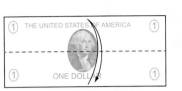

Start with George side up. Fold in half. Unfold.

2

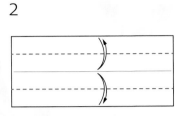

Fold the edge to the center. Unfold. Turn over.

3

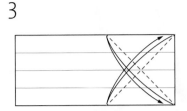

Fold the diagonals. Unfold.

4

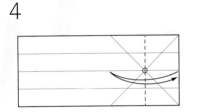

Fold at the intersection point indicated. Unfold.

5

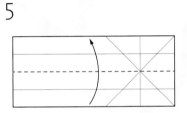

Fold in half.

6

Fold the edge to the crease.

7

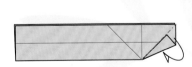

Mountain fold using the existing crease.

8

Fold the edge to the crease.

9

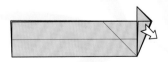

Make all the creases sharp. Unfold everything.

10

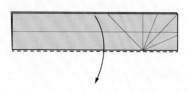

Unfold.

11

Valley fold between the points indicated.

12

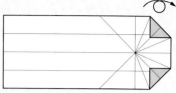

Turn over.

13

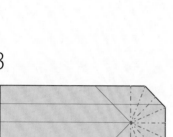

Reinforce the creases as mountain folds.

14

Fold the mountain crease to mountain crease, bisecting the angle with a valley crease.

15

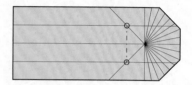

Mountain fold between the intersection point indicated. Unfold.

16

Mountain fold between the points indicated. Unfold.

17

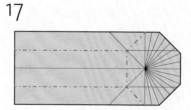

Reinforce the mountain creases indicated.

18

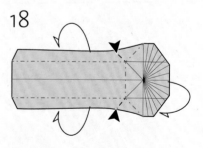

Fold the flap to behind and squash to make it flat. See next step for expected result.

19

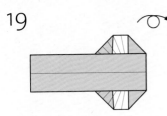

Turn over.

20

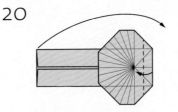

Fold the edge to the line, allowing the long flap on the back to flip out. Note: the model will not lie flat on the back.

21

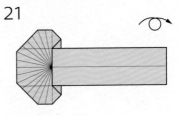

Turn over.

22

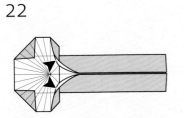

Squash fold, making the model flat.

23

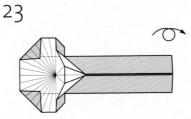

Turn over.

24

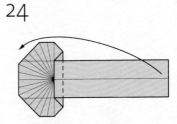

Valley fold by the edge.

25

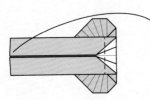

Fold the flap back, slightly above the edge.

26

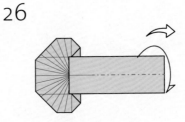

Partially mountain fold in half, leaving the tail three-dimensional.

27

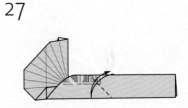

There are no precise reference points. You can use the printed pattern by the "E." Valley fold a diagonal. Crease well. Unfold.

28

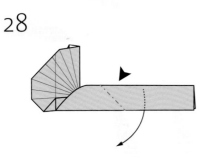

Reverse fold.

29

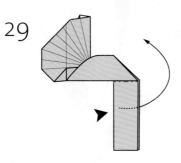

Open the flap slightly and reverse fold, corner to corner.

30

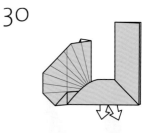

Carefully pull out the paper from inside.

31

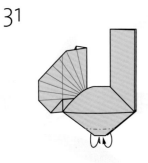

Mountain fold the bottom inside, in front and on the back. You can use the white part of the print of the dollar bill as a reference.

32

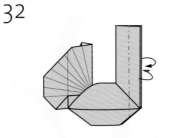

Open the flap slightly. Fold the edge to the center in front and on the back.

33

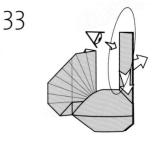

Open the flap and view from the top.

34

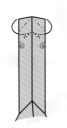

Fold the edge to the center, like the tip of the airplane fold.

35

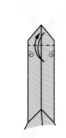

Valley fold, slightly below the corners. Unfold.

36

Rabbit ear fold, to create the beak.

37

Mountain fold and unfold using the swirls as a reference.

38

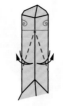

Lightly valley crease as indicated.

39

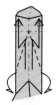

Crimp fold using the creases created in the previous steps and mountain fold the entire head and neck in half. Adjust the position of all creases and flatten.

40

Squash the neck area. Shape the feathers.

41

Turkey completed.

Walrus

The Walrus and Seal (page 105) models are great examples of how a design can be modified to create a whole new model. I originally designed the Walrus, then the next day I designed the Seal with a slight modification.

1

Start with George side up. Mountain fold in half. Unfold.

2

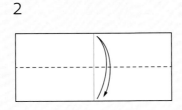

Fold in half. Unfold.

3

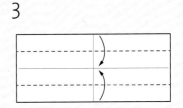

Fold the edge to the center.

4

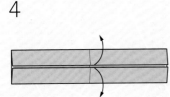

Unfold.

5

Unfold. Fold the edge to edge.

6

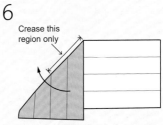

Crease only where indicated. Unfold.

7

Fold and unfold, similar to the last two steps.

8

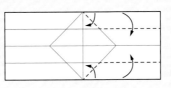

Reinforce the creases, in preparation for the squash. The model will not lie flat.

9

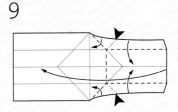

Fold the flap to the opposite side and squash to make it flat. See next step for expected result.

10

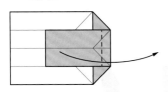

Fold the flap. There is some paper that will not lie flat.

11

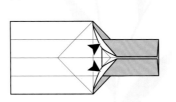

Squash fold to make the model flat.

12

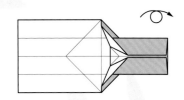

Turn over.

13

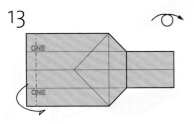

Mountain fold closer to the "N" of "ONE." Turn over.

14

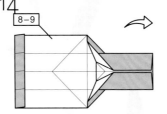

Repeat steps 8 to 9 on the other side.

15

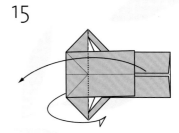

Mountain fold, allowing the flap to flip out.

16

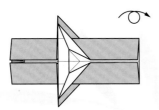

Turn over.

17

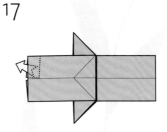

Pull out the corner from the inside.

18

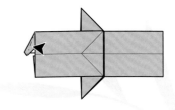

Create a mountain crease, corner to corner, and squash to flatten.

19

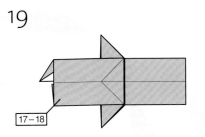

Repeat steps 17 to 18 on the other side.

20

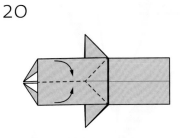

Rabbit ear fold, using the existing creases. The model will not lie flat.

21

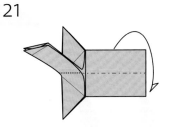

Mountain fold in half. The model will be flat now.

22

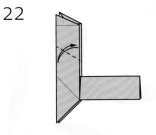

Fold and unfold all layers to pre-crease.

23

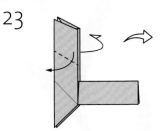

Outside reverse fold.

24

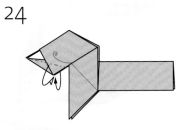

Mountain fold the corners inside the layers.

25

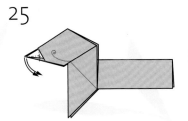

Rabbit ear fold, to shape the two tusks.

26

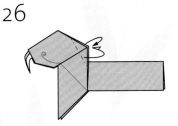

Mountain fold the corners inside the layers.

27

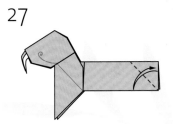

Fold the edge to edge. Unfold.

28

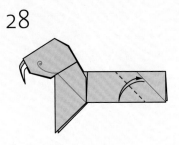

Fold and unfold.

29

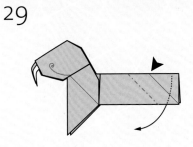

Reverse fold.

30

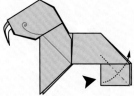

Reverse fold.

31

Open the fore-flippers and hind-flippers to make it stand.

32

Walrus completed.

Fun fact: Any damaged or torn dollar bills can be exchanged at your local bank if there is clearly more than one-half of the original note remaining.

ADVANCED MODELS

Mermaid

Half fish, half human; all cash.

1

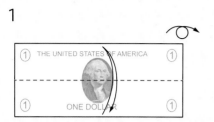

Start with George side up. Fold in half. Unfold. Turn over.

2

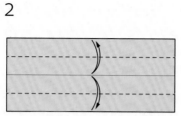

Fold the edge to the center. Unfold.

3

Mountain fold, using the printed pattern as a reference.

4

Using the printed pattern as reference, valley fold the corners as indicated.

5

Mountain fold in half.

6

Using the printed pattern as reference, fold and unfold as indicated.

7

Using the printed pattern as reference, fold and unfold as indicated.

8

Fold between the points indicated. Unfold.

9

Pivot from the point indicated. Fold the edge to the diagonal line. Unfold.

10

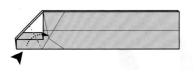

Reverse fold.

11

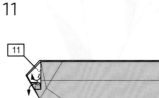

Swivel fold. Repeat on the back.

12

Valley fold.

13

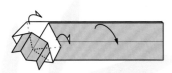

Open the model slightly. Mountain fold the creases created on step 8. Note: the model will not lie flat.

14

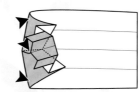

Pivot the head using the crease created on step 7, reverse folding it. Squash to make the model flat.

15

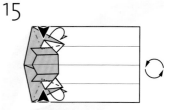

Mountain fold the corner to the back, incorporating a small reverse fold. This should leave only the head exposed. Rotate.

16

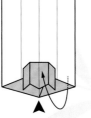

Sink the corner indicated and wrap around the paper from behind.

17

Valley fold, under the neck.

18

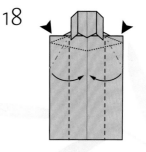

Fold the edges to the center. Squash on the top to make it flat.

19

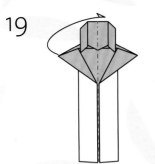

Mountain fold in half.

20

Fold and unfold, as indicated.

21

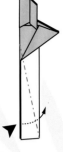

Reverse fold, using the creases created on the previous step.

22

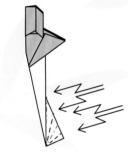

Repeat sequence of inside reverse until it is all between the layers.

23

Unfold. Note: the model will not lie flat.

24

Valley fold to shape the hair. Narrow the arms. Shape the body. Squash and open the fins. Shape to your taste.

25

Mermaid completed.

Shooting Star

Shoot for the stars with this shooting star. It can be a bit tricky to get this looking just right, but when you finally do it'll be worth showing everyone your shooting star.

1

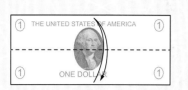

Start with George side up. Fold in half. Unfold.

2

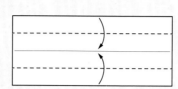

Fold the edge to the center.

3

Fold the raw edge to the folded edge. Create pinch marks by the edge, about an inch long, creasing it well. Unfold.

4

Pivot from the center, fold the corner on the line. Crease well. Unfold.

5

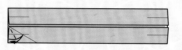

Fold edge to the line. Crease well. Unfold.

6

Reverse fold using the creases created on step 4.

7

Reverse fold using the creases created on step 5.

8

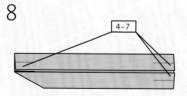

Repeat steps 4 to 7 on the remaining three corners.

9

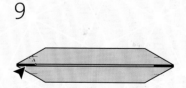

Open the flap and squash, creating one of the points of the star. Try to evenly distribute the 3 points on one side and 2 on the other, in the next steps.

10

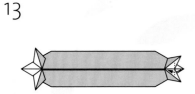

Repeat the open squash on the other corner.

11

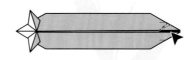

Open the flap and squash. Note the expected result on the next step.

12

Repeat the open squash on the last corner.

13

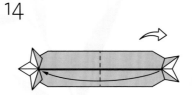

Fold the corner inside, hiding the point.

14

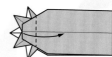

Fold in half so that the center of the points match.

15

Fold where the corners meet.

16

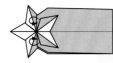

Rearrange the layers, to bring the points to the top, forming the star.

17

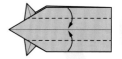

Turn over.

18

Fold the edge to the center.

19

Mountain fold in half, bringing all layers together. Rabbit ear fold by the center of the star.

20

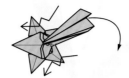

Crimp fold by the center of the star, aligning the tail.

21

Turn over.

22

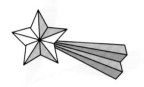

Shooting Star completed.

T. Rex

T. rex, complete with teeth. This is one of my favorite models. I initially thought I wouldn't be able to fold teeth into the T. rex because of how tiny the area surface of the paper already is, but was happily surprised when I discovered it wasn't too hard to add them.

1

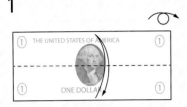

Start with George side up.
Fold in half. Unfold. Turn over.

2

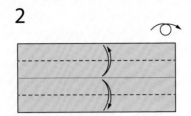

Fold the edge to the center.
Unfold. Turn over.

3

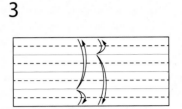

Fold edge to the line. Unfold.

4

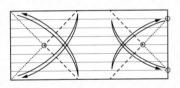

Fold the diagonals and crease where indicated. Unfold.

5

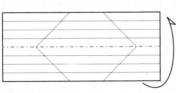

Mountain fold in half.

6

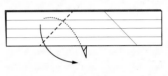

Outside reverse fold using the existing creases.

7

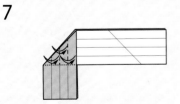

Holding the paper so that it will not shift, fold and unfold where indicated. This will create new creases between the layers.

8

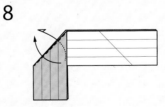

Unfold the outside reverse fold.

9

Repeat steps 6 to 8 on the other side.

10

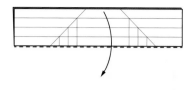

Unfold.

11

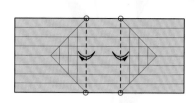

Fold and unfold between the points indicated.

12

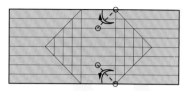

Fold the edge to the line between the points indicated. Unfold.

13

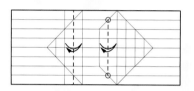

On the left, use the existing crease to extend to the edges. Unfold. On the right, valley fold between the points indicated. Unfold. Turn over.

14

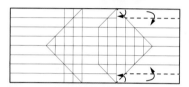

On the left, use the existing crease to extend to the edges. Unfold. On the right, valley fold between the points indicated. Unfold.

15

Reinforce the creases in preparation for the squash. The model will not lie flat.

16

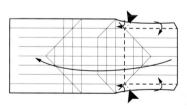

Fold the flap to the opposite side and squash to make it flat. See next step for expected result.

17

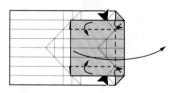

Repeat the similar procedure as the last two steps and fold the flap to the opposite side.

18

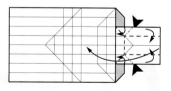

Repeat the similar procedure and fold the flap to the opposite side.

19

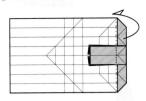

Mountain fold, allowing the flap to flip out.

20

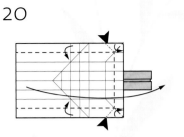

Squash and fold the flap to the opposite side.

21

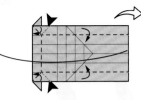

Squash and fold the flap to the opposite side.

22

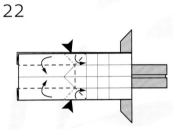

Squash and fold the flap to the opposite side.

23

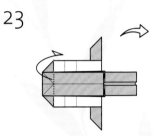

Mountain fold, allowing the flap to flip out.

24

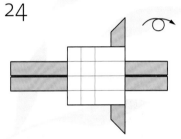

Turn over.

25

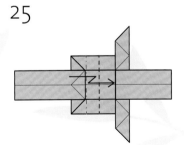

Pleat fold.

26

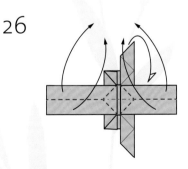

Rabbit ear fold the left and right flaps, and fold the model in half. The model should lie flat at the end.

27

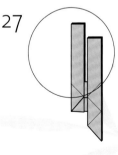

Details of the head next.

28

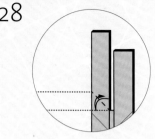

Fold the flap perpendicularly. Crease well the multiple layers. Unfold.

29

Outside reverse fold, distributing and evening the layers.

30

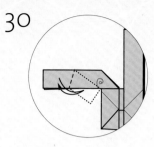

Fold corner to edge. Unfold.

31

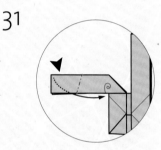

Reverse fold, distributing the layers evenly.

32

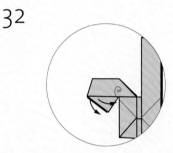

Swivel some of the four corners inside, so that they become separated.

33

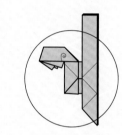

Details of the hands next.

34

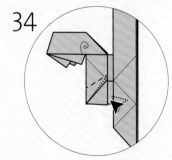

Push the corner and squash fold. Repeat on the back.

35

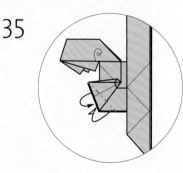

Fold the corners inside.

36

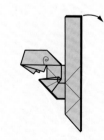

Pivot the tail slightly.

37

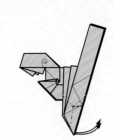

Rabbit ear the legs.

38

Fold the legs forward.

39

Crimp fold the tail.

40

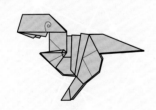

Fold and unfold all the layers.

41

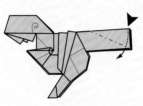

Reverse fold the layers evenly.

42

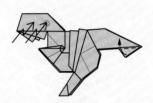

Tuck the corners between the layers, locking the tail. Pleat teeth so they stick out less.

43

T. rex completed.